SIMPLE
COURTESIES

SIMPLE COURTESIES

How to be a kind person in a rude world

JANET GALLANT

THE READER'S DIGEST ASSOCIATION, INC.
PLEASANTVILLE, NEW YORK / MONTREAL

A **Reader's Digest Simpler Life**™ Book

Designed by Lisa Feldman Design

Cataloging in Publication Data has been applied for
from the Library of Congress.

ISBN 0-7621-0062-1

Printed in the United States of America

CONTENTS

ACKNOWLEDGMENTS

While writing this book, I had the good luck to be connected to many kind and talented people. I'm especially grateful to Joseph Gonzalez, Deborah DeFord, and Henrietta Stern at Reader's Digest for their support and encouragement; Lisa Feldman for her lovely design; Nina Graybill for getting this project started; Robin Goldstein for her unfailing friendship, patience, and help; my wonderful sons Daniel and Michael Gallant; and my husband Andrew Gallant, my partner in all things.

For my mother and father, with love.

INTRODUCTION

In our hurried lives, we all want to feel good about how we relate to others. We'd like to be thoughtful and loving to those we're closest to, and courteous to people at work and in public. But everyday pressures often get in the way. We encounter rudeness and aggression, and at times we respond in kind. We may speak harshly to family, put off calls to friends, or behave abruptly in stores or offices. None of us likes acting in ways that make us feel embarrassed, defensive, or regretful. We'd much rather be competent and polite. The trouble is, we often don't know what to do. Our lives are so complex that most of the rules we bring to adulthood simply don't offer enough help.

The Golden Rule is an exception. "Do unto others as you would have them do unto you." *Simple Courtesies* is a reminder of why these age-old words of wisdom deserve a central place in our lives. They have stood the tests of time across the world's great cultures and religions because they offer a practical, effective, and moral way for people to get along with each other. When we answer the question, "How would *I* like to be treated?" we also answer the question, "What should I do?"

The Golden Rule gives us a consistent frame of reference, a model to follow when we're unsure of how to deal with people. As we apply this traditional principle, we gain a greater measure of control over our behavior and act in a more purposeful, caring, and confident way. The Golden Rule can keep us from losing our temper, enable us to relate more effectively to our children, make us more productive at work, and help us repair strained relationships.

Use *Simple Courtesies* to take a new look at the Golden Rule. You'll find here contemporary versions of the familiar concept, thoughts to reflect on, and suggestions for everyday use. The book does not present the Golden Rule as the solution to all our problems, but rather as an overall approach to personal interactions. *Simple Courtesies* is a practical, realistic look at how the Golden Rule can simplify and strengthen our relationships, and guide us effectively through the ordinary and extraordinary circumstances of our lives.

CHAPTER 1

When one-on-one communication goes well, it's a lifeline connecting us to each other and letting us make a difference in the world. With our words we move through daily life, explaining ourselves, strengthening our ties to family and community, and passing our values on to our children.

Communication can also go wrong, though. Then it separates us from others and can leave us feeling misunderstood, angry, or regretful. Unfortunately, in our stressful, over-busy lives, negative interactions are often what we experience and come to expect.

We're spoken to abruptly in doctors' offices and in calls to the bank or insurance company. On the job, a supervisor may rudely dismiss our work. At home, family members vent their frustrations. In turn, we may speak rudely ourselves, voicing our impatience while waiting in lines or forgetting common politeness at work. When we're with family or friends, we frequently express irritation or talk only about problems.

We'd all like to do better than this. Our one-on-one relationships, from the most businesslike to the most intimate, are essential for our practical well-being, companionship, and happiness. The quality of our relationships depends to a great extent on how well we listen and talk. Whatever we do to improve communication will also improve our connections to others, making our lives fuller and calmer.

We can make a positive change by putting more time and care into the way we communicate. Instead of saying whatever comes to mind, ignoring people's feelings, or reacting defensively, we can adopt a more thoughtful, responsible approach: we can communicate with others the way we want them to communicate with us.

To do this, we have to take the time to listen attentively and show that people's ideas and feelings matter to us. We need to let people speak without interruption, and we need to focus on what they say. Listening patiently and carefully will help us understand and thus get along better with our spouse, children, parents, co-workers, and friends.

Taking time is also important when we speak one-on-one. Phone messages and quick, practical exchanges are not enough. To connect in a meaningful way, we have to share our thoughts and experiences. We particularly need to talk at length with our children; only slowly, through many conversations over many years, can we convey our deepest beliefs, values, and traditions.

We always need to give careful thought to how our words come across and what effects they may have on others. Many of the things we say are potentially powerful. The right words can help or persuade people, let us feel understood, educate and guide our children, and end conflicts. The wrong words can damage our relationships, cause anger, disrupt our work, or start a fight.

We can't always know which of our words will be the powerful ones that resonate for good or ill. One-on-one communication is affected by context, feelings, and what happens before and after. In addition, the effects of communication are often hidden or delayed. Still, the more aware we are of what we say and how we say it, the more likely we are to get it right — to be listened to and understood as we intended.

To communicate with care, we don't have to give up spontaneity or feel anxious about details. Applying the Golden Rule actually simplifies speaking and listening. Instead of reacting impulsively to each situation, we have a consistent, comprehensive, and thoughtful approach that lets us feel good about how we connect with others.

LISTEN THE WAY YOU WANT OTHERS TO LISTEN TO YOU

The people we're closest to often tell us, "You're not listening!" "You don't understand!" And frequently it's true. We hear their words, but we tend to think about ourselves and what we'll say next. We make quick assumptions and jump in with a response. Then we lose focus, show impatience, and look for escape. The message we give is, "What you're saying isn't important." But if we value our connections to people, we need to listen with care, first because we all want to feel heard and understood, and second, because we need the information and insight we receive in order to get along, learn, and love.

judgment
opinion
prejudice

REMINDERS

- If you're taking the time to listen, act as though you *want* to listen, not as though you're doing a favor. Focus on the speaker and ignore distractions.
- Show courtesy regardless of the speaker's age or position in life.
- Try to truly understand what's being said. Check to see if you've got it right by asking questions or paraphrasing the person's statements and ideas.
- When you care about the speaker, listen even to messages you'd rather not hear. You can learn from words that are honest or heartfelt.
- If you're hurt by what someone says, consider the context and what you know of the person before assuming that harm was meant.
- As much as possible, don't let a harsh, angry speaker provoke or control you. Don't reward a verbal bully by admiring the power he or she may gain through the intimidation of others.
- Compliment or thank those who are consistently thoughtful speakers.

TALK AS YOU WOULD LIKE OTHERS TO TALK TO YOU

We've all been on the receiving end of rudeness and condescension, and we know that these ways of speaking can make us feel hurt, angry, and uncooperative. Yet we sometimes forget this, especially when we're rushed or when we feel safely anonymous or somehow "superior" to the people we're with. We may brusquely tell a waiter, "Get me more coffee." If our job involves serving the public, we may impatiently say, "Just wait in line like everybody else." We generate a lot of ill will when we adjust our level of civility to our mood or to what we think is our listener's worth. Communication is more effective, consistent, and appreciated when we simply show the same polite respect to everyone.

REMINDERS

- Before you speak, think about the impact your words might have on your listener. Consider the effect even of off-hand remarks and jokes.
- Use a tone of voice and body language that fit the situation and your relationship to the listener: businesslike, casual, familiar.
- Stay focused on your listener rather than looking around the room or shifting your attention.
- Keep your message brief, clear, and to the point, especially when you're giving information.
- Make your words interesting: use creative language, examples, anecdotes, and, when appropriate, humor and lively movements and expressions.
- Don't lecture your listener or monopolize the conversation.
- Watch for clues to how your words are received. Your listener's expressions and attitude will tell you when to explain a point, say more, or stop.

GIVE AND ACCEPT COMPLIMENTS
AS YOU WOULD LIKE OTHERS TO

Whether we have a lot in this world or a little, we can be generous with our words. There's always something nice to say. We can compliment an achievement, an effort, a look, an attitude, or a way of behaving. Our praise can be spontaneous or deliberate, offered to brighten someone's mood or to give a little encouragement. A sincere and appropriate compliment is simply a kindness. We should keep that in mind, too, when we receive a compliment ourselves, since embarrassment may lead us to deny any praise. Out of consideration for the speaker, who intended only a thoughtful gesture, we just need to say a simple "thank you."

- ❀ Offer a compliment when it has a nice and sincere thought behind it. Don't use kind words to deliver veiled criticism or manipulate others.

- ❀ Give a compliment that's appropriate to the relationship, not one that's too personal. Don't refer to someone's face, body, or overall appearance unless you know the person well and feel sure the remark will be taken positively.

- ❀ When you single someone out for a nice word, particularly a child, be aware of others standing nearby. You don't want to hurt them by leaving them out.

- ❀ If you get an appropriate compliment, assume that it's sincere and accept it graciously, even if that's difficult to do.

- ❀ Resist the temptation to talk about your faults or downplay your accomplishments, especially when a compliment comes from someone you don't know well.

OFFER AND TAKE CRITICISM AS YOU HOPE OTHERS WILL

Everyone has a hard time accepting criticism. We feel defensive, upset, and angry — less so if the criticism involves something we can and would want to change, more so if the criticism seems like an attack. Keeping our own sensitivity in mind can help us be more careful about what we say to others. If criticism contains important and useful information, it's worth offering or listening to. But if it's harsh and given simply to vent anger, it should go unsaid or unheeded. We encounter enough hurt in daily life; we don't need to purposely inflict more.

REMINDERS

- If you truly believe your criticism will help, and if the message is one you would want to hear if the situation were reversed, say your piece.
- Pick your words carefully and think about their effect. Be straightforward and respectful; don't speak in anger. Give your message privately.
- Don't unfairly criticize people who, because of their relationship to you, can't effectively answer back: your children, your employees, people who serve you in offices or stores.
- If someone you care about has a sincere criticism of you, hear it out. You need to know what he or she thinks, even if you don't agree with what's said.
- If someone's criticism is spiteful and gratuitous, don't respond on the same level. Speak calmly or end the exchange. If the speaker is someone in authority and you can't get away, learn what you can from the situation, even if only how not to treat others.

CHAPTER 2

Our lives can be tough on friendship. Although we're happiest with a variety of friends and acquaintances, we don't always connect the way we'd like to, especially during our most active work and childrearing years. Families and schedules keep us focused on present necessity: "What do I have to do now?" We work, take care of the kids, meet our obligations, and then retreat if we can, often just to watch TV—not to call a friend or meet someone new. We may get together with others on a weekend, and certainly we hope that our friendships will last. But we know that without effort and energy, they can fade.

We really need our friends, though, particularly during hectic or stressful times. They help us along by listening, advising, supporting, or simply diverting us. Friends want to be with us, so we feel valued and accepted, and because we can help them, we feel needed and useful in return.

When our daily routines confine us, friends widen our world. What they've experienced, we experience through them, and we can add their knowledge to our own. With their companionship or encouragement, we're more likely to take a risk and try something new. We're also more likely to have fun.

Most important, we go with friends through the ordinary events and the happy and sad milestones in each other's lives. The accumulation of shared experiences weaves us together. Ultimately, our closest friendships become a sanctuary, a safe place to go in any circumstance.

Making and keeping friends is important, lifelong work. Even when we're busy elsewhere, we need to put effort into staying in touch and treating our friends as we hope they will treat us. We all want the same thing—to feel connected in a satisfying way. The connection can take any form that works, from periodic calls to notes to frequent get-togethers.

We also need to extend ourselves to people who could become our friends. Although we may be happy with our own group, that group will inevitably get smaller over the years. Friendship isn't static. People come to us and then leave—or are left by us—for many reasons. Some relationships fade because shared interests or circumstances change; we no longer work in the same office, take the same classes, or have children in the same school. We lose some friends for reasons we can't control: they move out of town, or sometimes, sadly, become ill or die. If someone new approaches us, we should be kind, remembering how it feels to be the newcomer, and we should be open to the possibility of another connection.

If we aren't approached, and especially if we're lonely or would just like more companionship, we can actively seek new friends. Most of us look first to people who are like us. But if we cast our net wider, we can find friends who are younger or older, of another race or religion, on a different path, or with a different outlook. Such connections enrich our lives the way all friendships do while also offering us a greater-than-usual opportunity to be interested and interesting.

Wherever and however we look for friends, we'll likely have to make the first move, be patient and tolerant, and do more than our share for a while until others get to know us. At busy or difficult times, it's as hard to do these things as it is to keep in touch with long-term friends. But the effort is worthwhile and necessary. The energy we put into friendship now can help us find companionship, comfort, and support just when we really need it.

TREAT ACQUAINTANCES THE WAY
YOU WANT TO BE TREATED

We look to acquaintances for simple relationships and cordial encounters.

Acquaintances touch our lives, though our contact is limited. They may be neigh-

bors, coworkers, fellow commuters, employees in the stores where we shop,

or parents of our children's friends. By unspoken agreement, we keep our associa-

tions light, talking simply for fun or to share information and pass the time. An

acquaintanceship may not seem significant, but having a network of acquaintances

offers many rewards: the exchange of greetings when we're out, a conversation at

the office, company at our children's activities, and the continuing sense that we're

recognized and connected as we move through our day.

REMINDERS

---

* Extend yourself to others in appropriate settings: at work, at school, in the neighborhood. Smile, say hello, see if your greeting is welcome. If you're approached in the same way, respond politely.

* Respect personal boundaries and expect the same in return. Don't ask prying questions; don't feel pressured to answer them.

* Only request the kinds of favors you'd be happy to return.

* Realize that acquaintanceships can't substitute for the deeper bonds of close friendship. Don't seek strong support or reveal too much about your personal life. For long-term closeness, turn to people you know well.

* If you'd like to know an acquaintance better, strengthen your relationship slowly and mutually. Share brief conversations over a cup of coffee; gradually spend more time together, call each other, meet for lunch.

BE THE GOOD FRIEND
YOU WOULD LIKE TO HAVE

The best friendships are both strong and fragile. They sustain us in the most difficult times, but they require a careful and sensitive balancing of needs and expectations. From moment to moment, these relationships are never equal. When our friend has a problem, we put our own needs aside for a while. On another day we ask for support and trust that our friend will be there. The desire for closeness also varies. Sometimes friendship is a high priority. At other times we're occupied by work or family, and we pull back. The closest friends take the long view — they know that through give-and-take over time, each will feel valued, appreciated, and cared for.

REMINDERS

* Be trustworthy—don't betray a confidence or in any way deceive your friend. Follow through on your commitments.

* Be available to listen and help. Suggest ways your friend can deal with problems, but don't pressure him or her to follow your advice.

* Bring as much as you can to the relationship—insights, suggestions, interesting news, ideas for activities.

* Keep to a level of emotional intimacy that fits the closeness and nature of the relationship. Don't hide your feelings unnecessarily; don't tell too much.

* Be thoughtful and caring, and show a generous spirit. Be glad for your friend's successes and share your own; accept your friend's other relationships graciously, without jealousy.

* Be fair—don't ask for too much or insist on getting your way. Likewise, don't let yourself be imposed on.

TREAT FARAWAY FRIENDS AS
YOU WOULD LIKE THEM TO TREAT YOU

Few things are sadder than saying goodbye to a good friend, particularly if we've

known each other for years, lived together as roommates, or raised our children

together. After all the time spent talking, sharing, and counting on each other,

the day-to-day closeness ends, and there's no real comfort for the loss. While the

friendship may continue long-distance, its nature will inevitably change. Still,

strong friendships have a solid foundation of respect, affection, shared history,

and common beliefs. With our faraway friends, we can build a new kind of

relationship based on that foundation, or we can simply find comfort and support

in what we had.

REMINDERS

* Be realistic about the effects of separation; don't put pressure on yourself or your friend to maintain the relationship as it was.
* To keep your friendship active, communicate often enough to feel part of each other's lives; use the phone if that's what you're both used to.
* Try to be present for each other's major life events.
* If your friend stops communicating, don't assume he or she has lost interest. Your friend may just lack the energy or discipline to stay in contact.
* If you lose touch, don't let guilt or embarrassment keep you from calling, even years later. Your friend will welcome the call, just as you would.
* Whether or not you communicate with each other, be grateful that the friendship came your way. Remember and talk about your friend, look at photos, and think about him or her often.

CHAPTER 3

Family life is intense, absorbing, painful, and rewarding. Most of the emotional drama in our lives—both good and bad—is provided by family. With parents and siblings we experience love, nurturing, anger, and rivalry. With our partner we find passion, comfort, and conflict, while our children awaken total devotion and a deep feeling of vulnerability. Through family, also, we most closely confront eternal, fundamental truths: the births of our children, the deaths of our loved ones.

Our relatives may or may not be just what we'd want. But they're the family we've got, and for our sake and our children's, we should work on strengthening family ties. This can be difficult, especially if our lives are busy and our relatives are physically distant or in some way estranged from us. However, in all but the most abusive or neglectful situations, it's worth reaching out because we need what family offers.

Our family provides us with permanent connections and a sense of belonging. We feel part of something larger than ourselves, a group that shares a history and traditions. We have a claim on our relatives, and they on us; even when our relationships are strained, we offer some measure of support and acceptance in times of need.

Of all our connections, the ones with family have the potential to give the deepest satisfaction and greatest continuity over the years. The jobs, activities, and ambitions that occupy us now may not be what we ultimately come to regard as the most significant parts of our lives. We're more likely to focus our pride or regret on the kind of parent, spouse, son, or daughter we've been, and on how we're thought of by the people we love.

To do right by our family and to feel truly connected, we have to make family life a high priority. Many of us treat time with relatives — even our spouse and children — as something we'll get to later, almost an afterthought. But the years go by regardless of whether we're there to witness and participate. Our children, nieces, and nephews grow up; our spouse, siblings, and parents continue with their own lives.

Instead of working extra hours or spending our free time on personal activities, we can watch our children's games and performances, talk more with our spouse, meet our parents for lunch, and make a call to an out-of-town sibling. We can be with our relatives, or at least contact them, during holidays and special events.

If we feel distant or estranged from a relative, we can make the first move to reconnect, even if we still disagree about old issues and ways to act. Reaching out shows maturity and feels no worse than being in a hostile relationship. We can contact our relative on a birthday or special occasion, then call occasionally to stay in touch. Our attempt may not revitalize the relationship. But if we're able to create an ongoing cordial exchange where there had been coldness or anger, we've added some harmony to our lives. If our gesture is rejected, we can feel good for having tried, and at some point we can try again.

Getting along with family always requires thought and effort. Often, we don't want to deal with the complexities. But if we turn away, we're missing out on opportunities for emotional engagement, companionship, new experiences, and an increased sense of connection. Being actively involved with family is simply an essential, irreplaceable part of a life fully lived.

TREAT YOUR SPOUSE AS YOU WANT TO BE TREATED

We all want to come home each day to a loving, supportive partner and a relation-

ship that's a refuge from the stresses outside. This is our hope when we marry.

If we're lucky, we may get what we want, but not before life teaches us that we and

our spouse can disappoint each other, that it takes work and determination to

stay together, and that stress can come from many directions. It's in the course of

learning these lessons, sharing experiences, and creating our family that we reap

marriage's true and lasting rewards: acceptance, understanding, comfort, and

well-tested love.

REMINDERS

- Commit to keeping your marriage strong—recognize that at times each of you will expend more effort and do more compromising than the other.
- Be respectful and considerate; even if you've been together for years, act pleased to see your spouse, give compliments, offer to do a favor, show that you wish your spouse well.
- Disagree fairly—don't always insist on being right. Try to resolve arguments rather than allowing them to fester; let some things go, even though that's difficult. Never use physical force or tolerate its use against you.
- Try to be supportive through difficult times. Encourage your spouse to be hopeful; assist in finding help for your spouse when it's needed.
- Accept your spouse, but encourage and reward positive change.
- Do things together and talk often. Help each other stay interested in the world, healthy, flexible, and open to new ideas.

TREAT YOUR PARENTS AS YOU HOPE YOUR CHILDREN WILL ONE DAY TREAT YOU

No matter what the quality of our relationship with our parents, we're permanently and inextricably bound to them. They're with us, if not in person then in our memories and in the attitudes, values, and emotions they helped create in us. Our feelings about our parents are surely mixed. We may love them dearly but question some of their actions. We may regard them with regret or anger but still isolate loving moments. As our lives and theirs unfold, we can do our best to stay purposefully connected, not just in a dutiful way but out of love, a desire to understand ourselves and them better, an attempt to salvage what we can, or curiosity about what else this profound relationship will offer.

REMINDERS

- Acknowledge your parents' effort and love. Appreciate and praise what they've done well; try to understand their mistakes.
- Once you've permanently left their home, don't remain dependent or burden them with your practical needs except in an emergency.
- Show an interest — ask about their activities and concerns and listen to their ideas and suggestions. Be courteous, but don't feel you have to agree with what's said or give in to unreasonable demands.
- Stay involved — spend time with your parents, include them in some of your activities, introduce them to your friends, share your news with them.
- Encourage a strong relationship between your parents and your children.
- Accept your parents' personal choices. Offer assistance, but don't impose your way of doing things. If your parents become quite ill or impaired, try to ease their way and help them maintain a good quality of life.

BE THE KIND OF PARENT YOU WOULD LIKE TO HAVE HAD

During our busiest childrearing years, we easily get caught up in the practical details of meeting our family's needs and dealing with immediate situations. Our attention is so much on the here-and-now that we often don't notice how time and our own words and actions are shaping our child's character. We want our children to become confident, happy, disciplined, loving, and able to defend and take care of themselves. But we can't help them toward these goals without consciously focusing on the long-term effects of what we do. It takes deliberate effort, time, love, and patience to guide our children and set them on a good path through life.

REMINDERS

- Continually show your children with words and actions
  that you love, value, and accept them. Make their welfare your
  highest priority.
- Give them steady guidance. In ways appropriate to their ages,
  remind them often of how to act, stop them from behaving badly,
  and teach them your values. Don't belittle them, hit them,
  or compare them to others.
- Give your children hope that their futures will be good and that
  they can overcome problems. Set the stage for an interesting life
  by involving them in sports, arts, science, and reading.
- Show each of your children equal love. Step in to stop sibling
  rivalry; pay more attention to each of your children so they'll feel
  fairly treated.
- As your children go off to attend college or make their own homes,
  respect their independence but continue to offer love, encouragement, help, and guidance. Make it easy and appealing for them
  to stay connected to family.

TREAT YOUR SIBLINGS AS YOU WOULD LIKE THEM TO TREAT YOU

Although we're connected to our siblings from birth to death, the nature of our relationships is usually set in childhood. If we like our siblings, we have peer companions for life, with the ups and downs of any close relationships. If we don't like one of our siblings, we have a constant, irritating reminder of our parents' — and life's — real or perceived unfairness. Avoiding contact won't keep us from thinking about our sibling. But time, maturity, perspective, and deliberate effort can allow us to form a polite connection and even find value in continuing family history and traditions together.

REMINDERS

- If you and your siblings get along, do what you can to strengthen your ties. Call and visit, get together for special occasions, plan trips together.
- If your relationship has been strained, try to create at least cordial bonds based on recent experiences, family activities, and polite conversations.
- Encourage contact between your immediate family — spouse and children — and your sibling's. The cousins may form warm relationships even if you and your sibling aren't close.
- If you disapprove of your sibling's choices in spouse, job, or lifestyle, avoid interfering. Be civil, stay connected, and only offer advice if it's asked for.
- If your sibling has been more successful in ways that matter to you, don't let jealousy or resentment keep you from staying in touch; try to focus on other dimensions of the relationship. If you've achieved more, be sensitive to your sibling's feelings; don't show off or try to arouse envy.

BE THE KIND OF IN-LAW
YOU WANT TO HAVE

We become in-laws at vulnerable times in our lives. If we've just married, we may be young, unsure of our goals, dealing with unresolved issues in our own family, and adjusting to our spouse. If it's our child who's married, we're facing the end of active parenting, our own aging, and uncertainties about our place in the new couple's life. Some worry or tension is inevitable. But we don't have to let that get in the way of our new relationship. We can extend ourselves, be positive, and remember that we're connected to our in-laws by mutual love for a person—spouse or child—we hold dear.

⚙ When your child marries, recognize that it can take years for your son- or daughter-in-law to feel truly comfortable and learn your family's ways. Be flexible, nonjudgmental, and patient.

⚙ Don't intrude on your child's marriage by criticizing, imposing your wishes, or forcing the couple to make hard choices. In all ways, be supportive, understanding, and encouraging.

⚙ As a son- or daughter-in-law, treat your in-laws with courtesy, take an interest in them, and show that you love and are good to their child.

⚙ Don't hamper your spouse's relationship with your mother- and father-in-law. Also, don't automatically adopt your spouse's attitude toward them, especially if it's negative; create your own relationship.

⚙ Include your mother- and father-in-law in your family and holiday activities, if possible; encourage ties with your children.

CHAPTER 4

There are some good deeds we all believe should be done: making hospital visits, calling friends who are ill, paying condolence calls, and doing one-on-one volunteer work such as delivering food to those who can't get out. We know these are worthwhile acts, yet we're often reluctant to do them. Sometimes we say we're too busy, but time isn't really the issue. A phone call can be brief, and volunteering can be done on a once-a-month or even once-a-year basis.

Most of us avoid these good deeds because, for many reasons, we're uncomfortable. No one has taught us how to help or comfort people in need, talk to a grieving friend, or visit someone in pain. We have no obvious source of advice, and television shows and articles offer few models to follow.

On even the most practical level, we're not sure what to do. If someone is ill or in mourning, is it better to call, visit, or write, and when do we do these things? If we visit, should we bring something? How long do we stay? When we volunteer, what kinds of help are appropriate and how should we act?

Even more worrisome, we don't know what to say. We're used to keeping our deepest feelings private and having others do the same. How should we respond when people who are experiencing misfortune express their anger or sorrow, cry in front of us, or ask, "Why did this happen?" Do we talk about the problems or avoid them? What if we say the wrong thing? If we're volunteering, do we speak in a personal way to the people we're helping? How involved do we get?

None of us likes feeling awkward or inadequate. So we often refrain from reaching out to people in need, even though we want to. Then we feel guilty and embarrassed. We may even go out of our way to avoid the people we've failed to contact, possibly hurting them more, losing their friendship, and making ourselves feel worse.

Our worries are understandable, but unnecessarily limiting. In fact we're all capable of being genuinely helpful and comforting to others and of figuring out what to do, even if we are feeling awkward. We should remember that people with problems are not different from us. And people experiencing a loss don't suddenly become strangers. The coworker whose wife has died is the same familiar person we've talked to for years. Although we may be uncomfortable, we can still talk to him, even in his sorrow.

As the years go by, misfortune will come to all our doors. Each of us, at some point, will look for support, help, and a kind gesture for ourselves or our closest family members. If we're unsure of how to approach or assist people, we can think of the Golden Rule and treat others as we hope they will treat us in a time of need.

This means, primarily, visiting or communicating in some way with those who are troubled, ill, or in mourning, and doing one-on-one volunteering when we see a need. We don't have to worry about what's "correct." And we don't have to solve people's problems, speak profoundly, or fill every silence.

All we have to do is let others know that they are not alone, that they are in our thoughts, and that we'd like to offer practical help. As long as we speak and act with sincerity and a kind heart, our words and actions, whatever they are, will be good enough.

TREAT THOSE WHO ARE ILL
AS YOU HOPE TO BE TREATED

We sometimes become impatient with people who have a long-term illness. We

want them to get better and return to their normal relationship with us. When they

remain sick, we can feel overwhelmed. If the ill person is not a relative or very

close friend, we may let the relationship go. Many people do this, but we'd feel better

about ourselves if we could accept our sense of frustration and loss and continue

to be loyal and caring. We don't have to get involved in medical issues or arrange-

ments unless we, the ill person, and the family wish it. We can maintain our

friendship simply by staying in touch.

REMINDERS

❊ When a friend or acquaintance is seriously ill, call or write to say, "I'm thinking of you." If you're unsure of the person's condition, check with a member of his or her family first.

❊ Call ahead to arrange a visit. Bring a small gift such as a book or music tape.

❊ When you're together, try to focus on the person you've known rather than on the person's symptoms, changed appearance, or surroundings.

❊ Let your friend say what's on his or her mind, whether it's light, angry, or fearful. You'll provide comfort by listening in a careful, accepting way.

❊ If your friend doesn't lead the conversation, ask about his or her family, interests, feelings about the news, or background. If your friend prefers not to talk, ask if you can sit quietly together while he or she rests or reads.

❊ Call, write, or visit again. If you'd like to offer practical help, ask your friend or your friend's family what you can do.

TREAT PEOPLE IN MOURNING THE WAY YOU WANT TO BE TREATED

We approach grieving friends knowing that we can't take away their hurt over the death of a loved one. Grief is a fundamental and inevitable sorrow. We can be of some help, though, by contacting or visiting our friends and letting them know how much we care about them at such a difficult time. We don't have to say anything profound — they may look to religion for wise and comforting words. We can be simple. "This is such a sad loss. I wanted to be with you and tell you how sorry I am." We can listen to our friends and talk to them about the person who died. And because mourning may last a long time, we can continue to communicate over the weeks and months ahead.

REMINDERS

---

* Call or send a card to your friend when you hear of the death. If you knew the person who died, say something kind and personal about him or her.

* Offer practical help — cooking, shopping, or driving — or just pitch in if you see a need. However, don't push the family if they decline your offer.

* Listen to whatever your friend wants to say; encourage your friend to talk about his or her loved one. Share your own stories if you knew the person.

* If your friend cries, just sit with him or her. Put your arm around your friend, or give a hug if that seems appropriate.

* If you didn't get in touch at the time of the death, you still can, even months later. Apologize and tell your friend that you were uncomfortable and didn't know what to say, but that you've been thinking of him or her. You'll feel better, and your friend will probably be glad you called.

BE THE KIND OF COMMUNITY SERVICE
VOLUNTEER YOU WOULD LIKE OTHERS TO BE

When we offer a helping hand, it's often best to think small. If we dwell on all the problems in our community, we may find it hard to get started. "How can I make a difference?" We need to remember that the people we help are much like us — we're all glad for any small improvement in our lives. If we can do household repairs for someone with a disability, tutor a child in math or English, or drive someone to religious services or a doctor's appointment, we've done some good in the world. Whether we're regular or one-time volunteers, working with a group or in the neighborhood, we and the people we help will be better for our involvement.

REMINDERS

* Treat the people you help with respect, regardless of their circumstances. Don't show pity or condescension, or act as though you're doing them a favor.
* Focus on what you have in common — goals, family, feelings about the community — rather than on economic or other differences.
* Be prompt and reliable and stick to your commitments.
* Be friendly with those you help, especially if you see the same people regularly.
* If you're volunteering as part of a community service requirement, act as though you want to participate.
* Follow the suggestions and rules of the people in charge; stay focused on your task.
* Don't be discouraged if your volunteer job doesn't suit you; keep experimenting until you find a good match.

CHAPTER 5

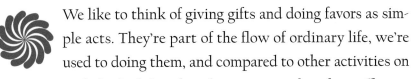We like to think of giving gifts and doing favors as simple acts. They're part of the flow of ordinary life, we're used to doing them, and compared to other activities on our overcrowded schedules, they don't require a lot of our effort or time. Yet, this small corner of everyday experience can cause us a surprising amount of stress and upheaval. Consider the pressure we feel when someone expects us to give a "perfect" present, or how we relive old hurts when a relative sends a "cheap" gift. A too-frequent request for a favor can leave us irritated and angry.

We rarely talk about these feelings. Their ungenerous nature embarrasses us, but the feelings are understandable. Giving and receiving close to home are not like other, more straightforward acts of generosity — contributing to charities, donating toys and food, and supporting religion or the arts. Giving gifts and doing favors intersect some difficult and sensitive personal issues.

One is our need for fairness. From our earliest days, we've compared our chores, possessions, and presents to our siblings' and friends'. As adults we still quietly measure what we give and do against what's given to and done for us and our family. If we send a present to our out-of-town cousins, we'd like a similar package in return. If a coworker repeatedly asks, "Could you pick me up on your way to work?" we'd like comparable help for doing the favor. But the balance of give and take doesn't always work out, often leading to unhappiness and resentment.

Our generosity is also complicated by our distaste for being put on the spot and judged. At times, we feel a great deal of pressure to give and to do it in a certain way. Our children may request presents that we don't think they should have or that are hard to find, guaranteeing an unhappy result. A friend may ask us to fill in for a babysitter when we want to relax with our family. Whatever we do in such situations, we can end up feeling frustrated as well as worried about the other person's reactions.

Add to this the issue of money. We're frequently unsure of what to spend on gifts and how to interpret other people's expenditures. Depending on our values and circumstances—and on whether we're giving or receiving—we may view an extravagant gift as a sign of great affection, simply what's expected, or embarrassing and manipulative. An inexpensive gift may seem sensible or rude and thoughtless.

The Golden Rule can simplify this area of our lives by helping us to focus on the act of generosity rather than on old slights and other people's motives and expectations. This may be hard for us. But we can choose to give and receive as we wish others would—reasonably and appropriately, with a kind heart and a desire to help and please. If we act in this spirit, we'll feel more in control of our emotions and better able to make good choices.

We will always have friends, acquaintances, or relatives who ask too much of us or appear unfair or ungrateful. We can try talking to them about our differences; we can consider stopping the exchange of gifts and favors with them. Or, especially with family, we can just accept their behavior, avoid getting emotionally entangled, and continue to do what seems right and best. As long as we conduct ourselves as we'd like others to, we can handle the sometimes difficult circumstances of giving and receiving in a consistent, thoughtful, and confident way.

GIVE GIFTS AS YOU WOULD LIKE THEM GIVEN TO YOU

We know that gift-giving should be caring and personal. But we can lose sight of this as we buy presents for birthdays, weddings, anniversaries, Christmas, Hanukkah, Mother's Day, Father's Day, graduations, and on and on. We give some of these gifts with obvious love, but others without much emotional involvement. We need to remember, though, that each gift marks a special event for the recipient, and the way we offer our present can add to or take away from the occasion and our own generosity. Whether we feel genuinely enthusiastic or not, for the short time it takes to give a gift, we should act delighted to be with and honor the recipient.

REMINDERS

- Offer a gift out of generosity—no strings attached. Don't use presents to unfairly influence others or as a substitute for love, attention, time, or respect.

- Avoid choosing a gift simply because you would want it or because you think the recipient should have it. Be guided by what the person seems to really like, even if the item doesn't suit your taste.

- Select a present according to your means, not the economic level of the recipient. If you're too extravagant or frugal, your gift may leave the recipient feeling guilty or resentful.

- Be satisfied with a simple "thank you." Don't look for strong or continuing expressions of gratitude.

- If you haven't received a thank-you note, don't automatically assume laziness or a lack of gratitude. The recipient may be appreciative but not disciplined enough to write, or may not have learned to make writing a habit.

ACCEPT GIFTS AS YOU HOPE
OTHERS WILL

People who give us presents want to make us happy, and we should treasure the kind gesture, separate from the gift. The gift itself may be disappointing — the giver might not have known or considered our taste, or may have been rushed and concerned about cost. Or the gift may be much more than we expected or wanted. Either way, the present was meant to please us, and we need to assume that the generous intentions are real. We can show gratitude for gift-givers' thoughtfulness and effort, and let them know they succeeded in making us feel valued and remembered. Our words of appreciation, our pleased attitude, and our thank-you notes are the small gifts we can offer to people who wish us well.

REMINDERS

- Have realistic expectations: don't pressure friends or relatives to buy you "great" presents; don't tell people not to give you gifts if you know they want to.
- Offer gift suggestions if you're asked, even if you'd rather be surprised. Remember that those who are asking just want to please you.
- Don't take generosity for granted, even when you're sure that certain people—your partner, your parents—will always give you a gift for certain occasions. Show that you recognize and value their thoughtfulness.
- In any situation, offer a quick, nice "thank you" for a present. If you like what you've been given, clearly show your pleasure. If you're disappointed, keep your feelings private and focus on the intentions.
- Send a thank-you note unless you're sure one isn't expected. Writing can be very difficult, but it's better to send even a barely-adequate note than to risk hurting and angering someone who's been kind.

DO AND ACCEPT FAVORS THE
WAY YOU WANT OTHERS TO

We often agree to do favors without expecting an equal effort back. If we like the

people who are asking, if they need us, and if we can do the job, we'll go ahead.

Our sense of accomplishment may be reward enough, or our satisfaction may come

from the company of the people we've helped or the belief that they'll lend us a hand

in the future. To feel good about doing and asking for favors, all we need is a sense

of balance and fairness in the relationship as a whole. Without this, we may feel

put-upon by unreasonable requests, and guilty and reluctant about asking for

assistance. With a basic trust in an overall relationship — whether at work, at

home, in the neighborhood, or among friends — we simply ask for and offer help

as needed.

REMINDERS

- When you've agreed to do a favor, be friendly and generous about it. If you act begrudging, your effort won't be appreciated.
- Follow through once you've committed yourself. If you've said "yes" to too much—either out of a desire to help or in response to pressure—do your best, since others are counting on you; try to be more cautious about future favors.
- Don't let yourself be repeatedly imposed upon. You can turn down a request without explanation.
- Don't ask for favors too casually or too often—recognize the amount of effort you're requesting; if possible, accomplish your task in some other way.
- Ask only for favors that are aboveboard, honest, and ethical.
- Be clearly grateful for a favor done. Even if the task appeared easy for the person, give full credit—the person may be keeping the difficulties or unpleasantness of the effort from you.

CHAPTER 6

Our social life can be a great positive force, raising our confidence and renewing our optimism and energy. While many of our daily activities leave us stressed and exhausted, getting together with people we like and love—whether dating, going to parties, or meeting informally—can improve our outlook and lighten our load. When we have a satisfying social life, we feel connected to a group of our choosing. We can find romance, enjoy ourselves, savor close companionship, and know that the resulting good feelings affect whatever we do.

We'd all like a social life that suits our personality and makes us feel valued and happy. Yet most of us, much of the time, don't have this. Hectic schedules, the difficulty of meeting new people, our own insecurities, and the sometimes harsh nature of personal relationships can all get in the way. Instead of being with close friends and romantic partners, we may find ourselves with people we don't really care for, in places we don't want to be, or just alone.

We can create a more enjoyable and satisfying social life for ourselves, although what's required—taking the initiative and reaching out more to others—can seem difficult or risky. However, if we extend ourselves to friends, romantic partners, and people we could become close to, the emotional rewards will more than balance our reluctance or anxiety. This won't necessarily happen quickly or smoothly. It takes practice to feel comfortable approaching people, issuing invitations, and entertaining. It also takes perspective to understand and accept that some disappointment is an inevitable part of getting socially involved.

We'll have an easier time reaching out if we know ahead of time how we want to act in social situations. Socializing, while usually pleasant, can sometimes bring out unexpected, competitive, and thoughtless behavior. We've all been to gatherings where our entrance and exit were barely noted or where we felt deliberately excluded. Unfortunately, we also, at times, may have been rude or uncaring ourselves.

In social encounters, we'll feel more at ease and sure of ourselves if we treat people as we hope to be treated, recognizing that everyone wants to be accepted and liked. Following the Golden Rule can help us approach a potential date in a friendly but not overbearing way. It can let us feel confident enough to introduce ourselves to strangers at a party, and it can guide us in making our guests or hosts feel comfortable and appreciated.

The Golden Rule can also help us base our actions on our own sense of what's right, not on what others do or think in social situations. Depending on the influences around us, we might be tempted to show off, keep up, or conform to people's expectations in order to fit in. We might also spend time with people because of their influence, wealth, or attractiveness, not because we enjoy their company. Acting counter to our values won't make us happy. We'll feel better about ourselves and form more satisfying social connections if we follow our good instincts and act with integrity.

At heart, what we want from our social life is almost touchingly simple: to be with people we like and love, and to know they're glad to see us. Although our time and energy may be limited, if we make the effort to reach out in a thoughtful and honest way, we can widen our social circle, find more enjoyment and love, and add greatly to our feeling of connection and belonging.

BE THE KIND OF GUEST YOU WOULD WANT TO HAVE VISIT YOUR HOME

An invitation is an honor. It means that someone who values our company is willing to plan for our arrival, prepare the house, cook for us, and think about our comfort. We need to appreciate the effort as well as the offer of hospitality. In return, we can arrive at our host's home ready to help create a good time. We can be friendly, interested in others, attentive to new people, courteous, willing to talk and share stories, and generally engaged in the proceedings. We need to do this for our own enjoyment and also for the sake of our hosts since they, like all of us, want to feel successful and appreciated.

REMINDERS

* Respond to an invitation promptly and kindly, whether or not you're accepting or the event interests you.

* Don't put your host on the spot with requests for special treatment — "I only eat low-fat food" — or last minute favors — "Can we bring our daughter?"

* Come on time and with enthusiasm. Bring a small gift you've chosen with the hosts' tastes or needs in mind.

* Offer to help, but be careful not to get in your host's way.

* Show that you're enjoying yourself. Get involved in conversation, be positive, compliment the meal.

* If you don't like the food, music, or company, deal with it discreetly. Don't say anything critical of or to your host.

* As you leave, be sincere in your thanks. Call the next day or write a quick note. Following up is a much appreciated kindness few guests take the time for.

BE THE KIND OF HOST YOU WOULD LIKE TO VISIT

When we entertain for the pleasure of our friends' company, we focus mainly on the comfort of our guests. When we host a special event—anything from a birthday to Thanksgiving dinner to a wedding—we also need to focus on the true meaning of the occasion. It's a privilege and a responsibility to oversee a rite of passage, a commemoration, or an ongoing tradition. If we emphasize and honor what's most important about the gathering, whether the event has cultural, religious, or life-cycle significance, we give our guests not only an enjoyable time, but one that's emotionally powerful and affirming.

REMINDERS

---

* Plan your event to please your guests; put effort and thought into making them comfortable and happy. Don't entertain simply to advance yourself, display what you have, or pay back obligations.

* Entertain according to your means, rather than your guests'. Whatever you have or do is fine, as long as you're gracious and prepare with care. Although it may be hard, don't let feelings of "inadequacy" keep you from entertaining.

* Welcome your guests sincerely, warmly, and individually.

* Act calm and glad to be a host. Avoid talking about the effort that went into the event, even if you did have to clean, shop, and cook.

* Throughout the gathering, pay attention to the flow of conversation and activity. If people seem left out, talk to them or involve them with others.

* As your guests leave, let them know you were pleased and honored by their company.

WHEN DATING, ACT AS YOU WOULD LIKE OTHERS TO

Because searching for people we'd like to date can seem emotionally risky or challenging, we often hide our real thoughts and feelings behind our "public" personality. We accept this about ourselves. But we don't show much tolerance for others who do the same thing. We tend to judge and often dismiss new people on a quick glance and a few words, without giving them the benefit of the doubt or getting to know them as we'd like to be known. We may miss out on many opportunities for connection and love this way. If we were more understanding and less critical, we might discover a nice acquaintance, a new friend, or a romantic partner we'd have been sorry to overlook.

REMINDERS

* Extend yourself to others, even if you're nervous. At gatherings, smile and act friendly; introduce yourself to at least one person.
* Be honest and dependable; call or show up when you say you will. Be considerate of your date's feelings; think about how your words may come across.
* Have realistic expectations. Don't look for perfection or premature commitment in a date; try not to be overly demanding or possessive.
* Don't pressure — or feel pressured by — a date to have sex. Follow your values and best instincts and avoid rushing into intimacy.
* Strengthen a relationship step by step, gradually sharing your feelings, experiences, and thoughts about your growing closeness.
* Maintain your own identity and interests, even when you're in love. If you have children, put your relationship with them first; be discreet about dating.
* End a relationship as civilly as you can, learn from it, and in time, try again.

CHAPTER 7

If we're lucky, we belong to a true community—a group of people we feel strongly connected to, who make us feel known, valued, and supported. Our community may be our congregation, or a club, school, or volunteer organization. Some of us find community in our neighborhood. But sadly, many of us feel isolated from the people who live around us, especially if we or they move frequently, or if we don't have young children to keep us involved with nearby families.

We'd like to feel recognized and "at home" in our neighborhoods. But we settle for isolation because our energy for fellowship is used up elsewhere—at work, with friends and family, in organizations we belong to, or simply in getting through each day. We tend to see our home as a retreat, or even a bunker, providing peace and shelter. We'd rather not have to chat before going inside, or get otherwise involved with people whose only connection to us is proximity.

Isolation from our neighbors has its appeal: it saves us the emotional wear and tear of making concessions and adapting to the needs of others. If we don't know the people around us, we're less worried about how we look when we go out, how our property appears, how our children act, and how much noise we make. In many ways, we can be more casual and relaxed.

Because day-to-day anonymity is easy, we'd have little incentive to change if we were happy. But we're generally not happy. We're embarrassed that we don't know our neighbors' names. We're worried that we have no one to turn to in an emergency. We remember our own growing up and feel guilty that our children live in such an impersonal environment. And no matter how strong our ties are to communities outside our neighborhood, we also want to make a difference and feel some connection to the people we live among.

We can meet our need for a neighborhood community and still keep a good measure of privacy by reaching out gradually, on a small scale, in a way that we'd like to be approached. Few of us will have the neighborhoods of our or our parents' youth, with the women at home and watchful, people aware of each other's comings and goings, and the children safely playing outside past dark. Our neighbors are as busy and jealous of their time as we are, but they also have the same longing for some contact.

It may feel awkward to make the first move and approach a neighbor, especially if we've had a merely nodding acquaintance for years. But we can talk about our discomfort. "We've lived on the same block for 2 years, but I'm sorry to say I don't know your name." We can spend more time outside so we have a chance for casual conversation, and we can make more use of neighborhood facilities like parks, restaurants, and shops.

Most important, we can slowly establish trusting relationships with some of our neighbors. We can start with a simple exchange of greetings, then small favors and longer conversations as we get to know each other. We don't have to aim for close friendship, although that may eventually come. All we need in our neighborhood are people we feel comfortable with and with whom we can share a mutually helpful and pleasant connection.

Community is good for us wherever we find it, whether in our church, synagogue, or other religious institution, in organizations we join out of interest and commitment, or in our neighborhood. Knowing others and being known and appreciated by them will always help us feel more firmly and happily tied to the groups we belong to and the place where we live.

BE THE KIND OF NEIGHBOR
YOU WANT TO HAVE

We always have something in common with our neighbors. In some cases, we're

friends setting down roots and raising our children together. But even in the

absence of personal ties, we share a common interest in the home ground we return

to each night — the buildings, parks, sidewalks, and streets surrounding us. We

all want our neighborhood to be safe and pleasant and to offer a decent quality

of life. Our well-being depends on how we treat each other and our immediate

environment. The farther beyond our door we extend our sense of caring and

connection, the greater and more fulfilling our stake in the community.

REMINDERS

- Talk to your neighbors. Start a conversation outside, give a compliment, or offer a cup of coffee. If someone approaches you, be receptive and friendly.
- Lend a hand when you see it's needed; offer to do a favor, and be someone to turn to in an emergency.
- Show consideration for your neighbors: respect their privacy, avoid being loud or disruptive, keep your property neat, and don't impose or ask too often for favors.
- Watch out for your neighbors' welfare. As you go about your activities, take a quick look at their children, their house, and their car to be sure all is well.
- Be friendly to—or at least tolerant of—neighborhood children and teens; don't assume they're bad kids simply because of their noise or appearance.
- Try to live with minor irritations caused by neighbors. Talk over bigger differences in a calm way; compromise and make getting along a top priority.

BE THE KIND OF ORGANIZATION MEMBER YOU WOULD LIKE TO SPEND TIME WITH

Everyone in clubs and organizations knows that parallel to the official proceedings is an informal flow of gossip, maneuvering, and personal politics. While some of us don't take part in this behind-the-scenes activity, many of us thrive on it. We form strong bonds with people who share our opinions, and we enjoy promoting our views or poking fun at absurd situations. The opportunity for close, interesting, intense interactions is part of the appeal of a voluntary organization. We need to remember, though, to be considerate and discreet with our comments and actions so our involvement doesn't hurt individual members or the group.

REMINDERS

❋ Recognize that people join your organization for diverse reasons, some primarily social, some related to a cause or interest. Be inclusive and tolerant of different personal styles and goals; welcome new members.

❋ Bring enthusiasm, openness, ideas, an ability to focus on the group's aims, and a desire to make the organization better.

❋ If you volunteer for a job, follow through. Be trustworthy and do your fair share; avoid taking on too much.

❋ Take your turn as a leader, support the leaders, or — if you disagree with them — discuss your concerns in a constructive way.

❋ Praise and encourage people who do a good job, put in extra effort, or simply show up consistently with a good attitude. If you're in charge of a project, call or write to thank your workers for their help.

BE THE KIND OF CONGREGANT YOU WANT OTHERS TO BE

A community of faith is not like any other. Whatever our degree of involvement as members, we're brought together by our shared beliefs and ethical values, and a commitment to pass our religious faith on to our children. Our congregation may seem almost family-like to us — a network of friends and acquaintances, people we like and don't like, fellow congregants and clergy we accept and in many cases greatly value over the years. As we witness the celebration or commemoration of each other's proudest and saddest moments, birth to death, we see God's presence in our lives and feel the comfort that faith and our communal place of worship can offer.

REMINDERS

❀ Consider your congregation a long-term community. Build close relationships with members. Be thoughtful, patient, and tolerant since you will be with your fellow congregants through the years.

❀ Encourage your children to feel comfortable and welcome in your family's house of worship. Involve them in rituals and celebrations; help them to learn about their religion and find the peace and strength that faith provides.

❀ Practice your religion in the company of fellow congregants. Worship, study, and celebrate holidays together.

❀ Participate in your congregation's volunteer projects, helping people in need and working for positive change in the community.

❀ Take part in some of the organizational work that supports congregational life — committees, fundraisers, governing boards — but don't get so caught up that you lose sight of your religious purpose.

CHAPTER 8

The school years are a precious opportunity for our children to gain knowledge and skills, pursue strong interests, and find joy and value in learning. What educators do and don't do to make these things happen is vitally important. When schools succeed in setting children on a path of life-long learning, all of us gain. But too often, and for many reasons, schools fall short in their central mission. Then, as parents, educators, or concerned members of the community, we have to encourage schools to do better.

Changes in curricula or policies are rarely possible at the local level, but there is one major improvement that everyone connected to schools can make. We can treat each other as we want to be treated. The simple application of the Golden Rule makes an enormous positive difference in schools, many of which—despite good intentions—can be unfriendly, uncivil places for employees, students, and parents alike.

Almost everyone involved in schools feels rudely treated at times. Principals deal with unreasonable parents, disruptive students, and teachers and staff who don't follow procedures. Teachers can feel under attack by parents and students, and unsupported by administrators. Office staff may feel unappreciated and overwhelmed by demands. Parents find teachers and administrators sometimes defensive and curt.

At the bottom of everyone's heap are the students. They're often treated in ways we would never tolerate in any other setting. Some of the rudeness is student-to-student, but some comes from teachers and other school staff who, dealing with their own stresses, tell kids to "shut up," embarrass them for making mistakes, forbid them to use the bathroom during class, and force them to sit silently for long periods despite all the evidence that kids learn best when they're active, involved, and trying things for themselves.

Schools would be more pleasant for everyone and more conducive to learning if those of us who worked there acted more consistently like the kinds of people we want our children to become: kind, patient, thoughtful, disciplined, confident, and focused on clear goals. Students working under such adults feel more cared for, inspired, and able to concentrate on work.

Certainly many students come to their classrooms with difficult life problems and negative attitudes. While those of us who are educators can't solve these problems—or the school budget and policy problems that also get in the way of learning—we can still try to meet our students with enthusiasm, understanding, a common-sense approach to discipline, and above all a determination to help them succeed academically.

We can also offer children and teenagers an invaluable life skill by teaching them to use the Golden Rule themselves. Some students lack the basic values they need to get along in school; most students need frequent reminders about behavior. The Golden Rule offers a simple way for students of all ages to figure out how to act.

A 7-year-old who hits his classmates may not know what he should do instead. But if a teacher asks him how he'd like others to show their anger at him, he'll likely find the right answer: "I want them to tell me, not hit me!" A teenager who laughs at people's errors in class can be asked privately to consider how she wants to be treated when she makes a mistake, and then encouraged to act that way around others.

The school years will inevitably leave our children with a foundation of knowledge, habits, and attitudes. The content and nature of these will depend in large part on the quality of life in school. If everyone involved in education teaches and lives the Golden Rule, our students will have a much greater chance to succeed.

BE THE KIND OF TEACHER YOU WOULD LIKE TO HAVE HAD

When we first sign on to teach children, we have a passion for our subject matter and a drive to help kids better their lives. We need to keep a measure of that enthusiasm all through our career so we can excite our students and engage them in learning. At times, we may be the only adults urging them to look at the wider world. We can spark our students' interest by relating schoolwork to real-life situations, taking class trips for the sheer joy of learning by doing, and talking to kids about the news, no matter what subject we teach. If our classes are lively and interesting, we'll feel good about teaching and our students will feel better about coming to school.

REMINDERS

- Base your teaching on a good understanding of children's developmental stages and different learning styles. Be flexible; use a variety of methods and activities to reach each child. Be creative and encourage student creativity.
- Model a good work ethic. Be on time, grade papers quickly, make your written comments understandable and helpful, and put effort into class plans.
- Challenge your students academically; don't talk down to them or give them busy work. Show confidence in their ability to learn and to figure things out.
- Be a good example of a kind, confident adult. Let your students know that you're interested in them and care about how they do.
- Be flexible about such things as where students sit or whether they talk in class. However, set firm limits on behavior that disrupts learning. Don't let students treat each other badly.
- Establish a working, cordial relationship with parents; encourage contact.

AS A PRINCIPAL, TREAT OTHERS
AS YOU WOULD WANT TO BE TREATED

Because administrators shape the character of their schools, they have the power to affect many people's lives in a positive way. If a principal encourages a friendly, cooperative atmosphere focused on learning, then students and faculty will feel safe and supported. Office staff will feel motivated to be polite and helpful, and parents will feel welcome when they visit or call. Although principals have many administrative tasks to perform, their most significant job is consciously setting the tone for the school. Educators, students, and parents all look to their principal for the kind of guidance, leadership, and direction that can make student success possible.

REMINDERS

- As an administrator, create a safe environment for learning. Don't allow threatening, profane, violent, or illegal behavior. But don't make the enforcement of routine restrictions, such as those on talking, using lockers, or being in the hall, a primary focus. Keep student learning as your main goal.

- Be firm about expecting civility from all. Don't accept student-to-student or teacher-to-student rudeness or cruelty.

- Spend as much time as you can in classrooms. Know what teachers are doing, support and encourage them, and get them help when they need it. Spend time with students in the halls, and at activities and games; greet kids by name.

- Help teachers feel they have a professional stake in the school: give them some real control over what and how they teach; consult them on policies.

- Treat parents courteously, even if they're confrontational; they just want what's best for their child. If you can't do as parents request, explain why.

AS A PARENT, SHOW EDUCATORS THE
RESPECT YOU WOULD LIKE TO BE SHOWN

The best thing we can do to support our children's educators is help our kids

acquire the outlook, skills, and enthusiasm of life-long learners. Especially during

the elementary years, our kids need our close watchfulness and encouragement as

they develop study habits, learn to do homework, and form basic attitudes toward

school. During the teen years, they still need guidance in focusing effectively on

school work. Although our children may not know what qualities will lead to

success in school, we know, based on our experiences, perspective, and even regrets

about our own education. We can give our kids a good start in school and in life by

helping them get ready and stay ready to learn.

REMINDERS

- Speak supportively of your child's teachers, take an interest in your child's school work, and encourage your child to make a good effort.
- Establish a working relationship with your child's teachers: come to scheduled meetings and individual conferences, and respond to calls or notes.
- If your child has a school problem, talk to the teacher, even if you feel nervous. There's very little risk that speaking up will make things worse.
- Speak to educators calmly and politely. You can be a forceful advocate for your child without being rude or losing control. Explain what you think your child needs, and listen to the teacher's side. If you're not satisfied and the issue is important enough to you, go to the principal or beyond.
- Show support by volunteering in the school, even if only once a year.
- Give your child's principal or teachers positive feedback when they've been particularly helpful or understanding.

BE THE KIND OF STUDENT YOU WOULD LIKE TO TEACH

It's useful, satisfying, and wise to learn all we can and take advantage of every educational opportunity. We tend to see this most clearly in retrospect as we get older and farther removed from our formal schooling. But we don't have to wait until we're done with school to appreciate the privilege of being a student. If we're in high school or college, we can recognize the real-life benefits of picking up skills and practical information. If we're older and returning to school, we can be grateful for another chance to learn. And if we're the parents or teachers of younger students, we can help them find the joy in physically and intellectually pursuing their curiosity about the world.

REMINDERS

- Read a lot. Television can tell you only a small portion of what you want and need to know. Books, magazines, and newspapers can tell you about anything.
- Engage in conversations with a wide variety of people. The better you are at listening and expressing yourself, the more successful you'll be.
- Learn enough about science and technology to understand the breakthroughs that will affect every aspect of your life.
- Ask many questions, both when you don't understand something and when you think something is wrong. Don't accept every answer you hear.
- Learn enough about history to feel connected to a long chain of people with different experiences, but with many thoughts and feelings similar to yours.
- Try doing tasks in creative ways. Look for unusual solutions to problems. Imagine yourself in different times, places, and cultures.
- In school, treat teachers and students with respect.

CHAPTER 9

We devote a major portion of the time and energy we have in this life to our work. We do this because we have to and because we need the sense of purpose and accomplishment that work can give us. Our simple and basic hope is to find a fulfilling job at a good wage. In reality, being employed is often a complex mix of benefits and problems. A job that satisfies many of our needs can still leave us with practical, financial, or emotional concerns.

Even if we like our work, we may have to deal with low wages, long hours, trouble with a supervisor, or a lack of job security. We may also feel pressure to keep our skills up, stay ahead of competitors, and satisfy clients or customers. And because work affects all other areas of our life, we may need to search for good daycare or elder care and struggle to make time for family, chores, and personal activities.

We accept some stressful conditions as the cost of being employed, and simply do what we must to keep working. At times, though, our job may take too much from us. A tense, demeaning, or highly pressured work environment can threaten our confidence, health, and family life. Then we have to make changes.

The most obvious move — quitting our job and finding a new one — is often not an option, especially if our skills aren't in demand or the job market is weak. We may have success requesting on-the-job improvements. But if our supervisors are not receptive or our coworkers are likely to react with hostility, this also may not be a realistic option.

Still, we can lessen job-related stress by changing our actions and attitudes. For our own sake, we can work as we'd like others to. We can find satisfaction and dignity in doing our job well, even if those around us don't fully appreciate our effort. We can create our own goals and challenges on the job, both to test ourselves and to stay stimulated and involved. And we can take pride in continuing to show up and put in a full day's work under difficult circumstances.

We also can remain hopeful and ready for positive change. Although we may not see possibilities for job improvement in the near or even distant future, we never know what will happen. If we simply resign ourselves to unhappiness at work, we may become too bitter and passive to look for opportunities. But if we sharpen and widen our skills and stay knowledgeable about our field, we'll be prepared to take advantage of openings and opportunities.

Finally, we can try to create a more realistic balance between work and the other areas of our life. If our job is tense or unrewarding, we can look more often to family, friends, and religion for emotional satisfaction, and we can turn to interests and hobbies to keep ourselves active, challenged, and connected.

If our stress comes from long hours at work pursuing ambitious goals, we can look again at what's most important to us. We may be spending too much time away from our spouse and children. Or we may have set family life and friendship entirely aside in favor of our job and its potential rewards, including money, possessions, and prestige.

The success we achieve at the expense of our personal life or loved ones comes at a high price. Ultimately, we'll feel happier if we invest our time wisely and fairly enough to sustain both job and family. Then, whatever we accomplish and experience in one essential area of our life —work or home —will complement and enrich the other.

WORK AS YOU WOULD LIKE OTHERS TO

We all want to feel proud of our effort and accomplishments on the job, and proud of the way we conduct ourselves. At times, though, there are conflicts between our values and the realities of our workplace. We may have supervisors who urge us to act in unfair or even unethical ways, coworkers who pressure us to do less or more than we feel we should, and demands made on our time that we can only meet by sacrificing our family and interests. It's important to fit in and be part of a team at work. But we still need to follow our own standards, values, and ideals. In the long run, our sense of self-worth depends on making the best choices we can and keeping our integrity, our essential nature, intact.

REMINDERS

- For your own satisfaction and the good of your workplace, give your best effort, even if the circumstances or rewards are not what you'd like.

- Have a cooperative attitude. However you feel about your job or other aspects of your life, don't act begrudging, negative, or resentful. Treat the people you work with in a polite, thoughtful way.

- Be fair, honest, and realistic in your dealings with others. Stay in touch with office politics, but don't participate in personal attacks. Understand that people will look after their own interests, just as you should look after yours.

- Be dependable and trustworthy. Stick to your schedule, use your time well, and follow through on your commitments.

- Take a creative, problem-solving approach. Don't wait to be told what to do.

- Learn new skills; be prepared for changes in technology and procedures. Stay up-to-date on developments in your field and in the news.

BE THE KIND OF SUPERVISOR
YOU WANT TO HAVE

If our job includes supervising others, we have a reliable, internal guide to being an effective leader: we can act as we want those who supervise us to act. Regardless of our position, we all want our supervisors to have integrity — to be competent, reliable, and hardworking, to treat us fairly, and to give us support and honest feedback. When we supervise others, the farther we stray from this model, the more our actions may become inconsistent, harsh, or weak. Then the people under us react as we would, with resentment, fear, and a reluctance to take a risk or put in extra effort. To encourage the best work from the people we're responsible for, we need to consistently provide the kind of leadership we'd like to have for ourselves.

REMINDERS

- Set an example by doing your job with care, energy, and honesty, following through on commitments, and staying focused on your work.
- Show loyalty to your employees. Back them up; support their good ideas and projects. Don't criticize them in public.
- Treat those you're responsible for as individuals, not replaceable, faceless workers. Be polite and friendly without being overly personal. Recognize that they, like you, have family and other obligations, and be realistic about demands you place on their time.
- Give clear direction and useful feedback, both positive and negative; explain evaluation processes and the consequences of not performing to expectations.
- Give your workers as much autonomy as possible. Tell them the outcome you want but give choices about how to do the work. Encourage initiative.
- Give credit, thanks, and, when fitting, financial rewards for a job well done.

AS A SERVICE PROVIDER, TREAT OTHERS THE WAY YOU WANT TO BE TREATED

When our job is to provide a service, the way we treat our customers, clients, or patients has both an immediate and a cumulative effect. In the short term, we influence people's moods and the success of their tasks and activities. In the longer term, we affect people's overall attitudes toward institutions and public life in general. Fairly or not, the perception of society as increasingly rude and harsh is based in part on encounters with employees of stores, restaurants, hospitals, and offices of every sort. Each time we do our job in a gruff way — even if we feel justified — we reinforce the negative view. Our power for good lies in doing our job courteously and efficiently and helping to create positive experiences.

REMINDERS

❀ Treat customers, clients, and patients as individuals with feelings like yours. Be polite and helpful; at times, do more than you have to.

❀ Respect people's privacy, especially if you handle confidential information. Use a private place or at least a quiet voice to discuss issues such as illness, employment, or bills. Never publicly talk about your patients or customers.

❀ Give people the benefit of the doubt. Don't assume they're going to shoplift, leave without paying, be late, or lie unless you have evidence.

❀ Listen thoughtfully to complaints. If you've made a mistake, apologize sincerely, offer just compensation, and attend to the source of the problem. If you're not at fault, still remain cordial, even though that may be difficult.

❀ If you're treated badly by a rude customer or patient, try not to take it personally or let it affect how you do your job. If you treat people well, you can take pride in doing your best regardless of how others act.

PUT THE THOUGHT INTO BUSINESS COMMUNICATION YOU WANT OTHERS TO

Much of business communication is unnecessarily alienating. Phone recordings frustrate us with endless instructions to "press 1, press 2, please hold...." Written reports ramble on, and many E-mail messages lack even basic signs of civility. Both as workers and members of the public, we often feel unheard and put-upon when communicating with companies and institutions. If we have the opportunity and we feel secure enough, we can give feedback about bothersome communications and offer suggestions for improvement. Always, we can communicate at work as we'd like others to — in a brief, clear, and polite way.

REMINDERS

- Make your business writing easy to understand, short, and to the point. Avoid jargon and dull, complex sentences. Proofread; correct spelling, typos, and grammatical mistakes.

- Communicate timely information quickly and clearly.

- Use simple phone courtesy: answer in a pleasant voice, especially if you receive calls from the public; avoid leaving people on hold; return calls made to you; try to be available to receive calls after you've left messages for others.

- Show the same politeness in an E-mail that you'd show in a business memo or letter. Write with care, and keep your message brief. Use a tone — professional, formal, or friendly — that's appropriate for the circumstances and recipients.

- In general, be sparing in your business use of E-mail, paging, faxes, and the phone; it's a kindness and a favor not to overload others with calls and messages.

CHAPTER 10

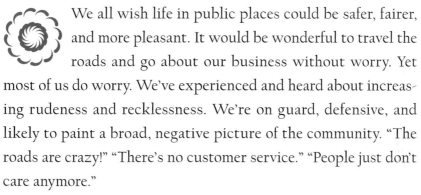 We all wish life in public places could be safer, fairer, and more pleasant. It would be wonderful to travel the roads and go about our business without worry. Yet most of us do worry. We've experienced and heard about increasing rudeness and recklessness. We're on guard, defensive, and likely to paint a broad, negative picture of the community. "The roads are crazy!" "There's no customer service." "People just don't care anymore."

Our feelings can cause us as much distress as the rude actions of other people. Consider the shock and anger we carry for hours after a shouting, selfish driver cuts us off, or the regret or shame we feel for overreacting to a slight. The worry, the bad behavior, and the resulting emotions all get in the way of using and enjoying our great public resources.

Life out in the community doesn't have to be this way. We can change our own actions and feelings for the better and influence the actions of others. To begin, we need to recognize that most people, most of the time try to do what's right. We give exaggerated importance to bad behavior because it's shocking and has far-reaching effects. It takes only one crying baby in a theater to upset 400 moviegoers, and one loud boom box to bother all the people at a bus stop. When we assess our communities, we should give law-abiding, responsible people their due. The trust we place in strangers is almost always justified.

Next, we can be more civil ourselves, treating strangers in public places as we'd like to be treated. We've all been guilty at one time or another of speaking harshly, ignoring people, taking an unfair turn, or being too impatient. Much of the time our rudeness just begets ill will and leaves us embarrassed or remorseful. If we follow the Golden Rule in public, the good we do may come back to us in a surprised "thank you" or a more pleasant encounter. Certainly we'll feel better about our actions and choices.

Another way to improve our public experience is to look at the reasons why people, ourselves included, sometimes treat others badly. The difficult problems many of us deal with—including worries about money, jobs, childcare, and family—can cause pressure, anger, and distraction. At times, the stress may spill over into thoughtless public behavior. None of us is immune.

Understanding bad behavior doesn't mean excusing it. But understanding can help us apply the Golden Rule on a deeper level, not just to the manners we use in public, but to the way we treat people in all areas of our lives. If we help each other feel valued, respected, and supported at work, at home, and in the community, we'll also help each other act more calmly and thoughtfully.

Finally, we can improve our community life by taking action against offensive or aggressive behavior. We don't have to respond in kind or put ourselves at risk to make a difference. If a person is exceedingly loud or disruptive in a public place, we can ask someone in authority to deal with it. If we're treated rudely by a store or business employee, we can tell the manager and take our business elsewhere.

In public places, we always have choices. When we choose to treat others well, encourage positive change, and recognize the connections between us—common goals, common problems—we feel better and more in control of our actions and emotions. We also help to make our communities more enjoyable and peaceful places to be.

IN PUBLIC PLACES, ACT AS YOU WISH EVERYONE WOULD

So much of our time is spent with strangers. We share roads and trains, eat restaurant meals side by side, and wait together in grocery lines and doctors' offices. The way we treat each other affects both our immediate well-being and our sense of connection to the world outside our homes. If we're rude or careless, we detract from community life and give those we encounter yet another reason to feel angry or distrustful. But if we're considerate and responsible, we enhance public life and help the people we come in contact with to feel more secure, respected, and reassured.

REMINDERS

- Speak politely to others. Smile and be pleasant if that fits the situation.
- Don't disturb people: talk quietly, use headphones for music, and minimize noise from a beeper, cell phone, or laptop computer. Avoid talking in places such as movie theaters, where we depend on each other's silence.
- Respect people's privacy and space. Don't sprawl out, get too close physically, or intrude on others' activities or conversations.
- Wait your fair turn in lines and in less formal settings such as at store counters and bus stops. Don't tie up phones, water fountains, or restrooms.
- Keep your children from being disruptive. Try not to put them in situations where they're likely to be a bother if they simply act their age.
- Be sensitive to people's difficulties. Offer your bus seat to someone in need; hold the door for a parent with a stroller.

RESPOND TO DISTRESSING SITUATIONS AS YOU HOPE OTHERS WILL

Disturbing things can happen in public, from uncomfortable encounters to frightening crimes. We want to take action or protect ourselves in bad situations, but we often don't know what to do, in large part because we worry that our reactions might cause further harm. We all fear the possible violence of strangers. Still, we don't have to feel helpless. Whatever the circumstance, we can do something to help with the immediate problem or at least to lessen the chance of future occurrences. We can offer or call for assistance, ask for better treatment, push for a safer environment, and every day, look out for the welfare of those who share our community.

REMINDERS

◉ When a stranger treats you particularly rudely or disturbs
people, speak up if you feel safe enough. If you don't feel safe,
ask someone in authority—a manager, a guard, a bus driver—
to handle the situation. If that isn't possible, call or write later
to ask for better supervision and protection.

◉ If you're treated badly by a store or business employee, let
someone in charge know. If you aren't satisfied, stop patronizing
the business and tell others so they, too, can avoid bad service.

◉ If you witness a fight or crime, act as you'd hope a passerby would
act seeing one of your own family members victimized. If it's too
dangerous to get involved, call for help right away.

◉ If you see an accident, offer assistance if you safely can and call
for help.

◉ Pressure businesses and government to make public places safer,
with more lights, more emergency phones, and more patrols.

DRIVE THE WAY YOU WANT OTHERS TO DRIVE

Driving without traffic is a pleasure, but driving in heavy traffic is a stressful chore. When others cut in, we get angry. "They should wait their fair turn!" But when we're the ones in a hurry, we resent the selfish people who won't let us in. We need to be more careful with each other. Driving is not simply a routine means of going about our ordinary activities. Being on the road is a communal act of faith. We entrust our lives and our loved ones to the judgment and good intentions of strangers, and likewise, they depend on us.

REMINDERS

⊚ Don't abandon good manners when you're in a car; if you wouldn't yell or take unfair advantage face to face, show the same restraint while driving.

⊚ Follow the rules of the road. Wait your fair turn at lights and in lines.

⊚ Give others a break. Let someone in, leave room for turns. Wave your thanks when someone gives you a break.

⊚ Be cautious and patient around pedestrians and cyclists; remember how vulnerable you feel when you or your children walk or bike near traffic.

⊚ Don't do anything to make new or cautious drivers more nervous.

⊚ Don't take aggressive driving personally. Don't respond or retaliate. Rude drivers aren't targeting you—they'd cut in front of anyone in their way.

⊚ Try to be patient and detached when thinking of discourteous drivers. You don't know the reasons for their behavior, and we have all, at one time or another, made mistakes on the road.

BE THE KIND OF CUSTOMER YOU WOULD LIKE TO DEAL WITH

Sometimes shopping is fun. We're relaxed, interested, and in a good mood. At other times it's stressful: we're rushed, worried about money, unable to find what we want, or frustrated that the clothes we try on don't fit and that the check-out line is so slow. We have a similar range of feelings when we eat out: the service is either just right or too fast, slow, aggressive, or careless. Whenever and wherever we shop or eat, our styles and moods inevitably clash with someone else's. We need to be patient with fellow customers, salespeople, and waiters, and remember that we all share the same array of emotions, even if we experience them at different times.

REMINDERS

⊚ In stores, be considerate of the employees who straighten up after
you. Put items back on shelves and racks; don't mess up displays
and dressing rooms.

⊚ Don't talk down to salespeople or waiters or take advantage of
the fact that their job doesn't allow them to answer you in kind.

⊚ If you have a complaint, don't berate the person serving you.
He or she probably has little control over policies, costs, quality,
or refunds. Discuss the issue with a manager; present your side
calmly and clearly.

⊚ Be considerate of other customers. Wait your fair turn. When
you're ready to check out, have your items, payment, and IDs
ready; avoid taking up time with unnecessary questions, requests,
or discussions.

⊚ Don't cheat a store by making unfair returns. In addition to being
dishonest, this causes store employees to be more suspicious of
everyone and leads to higher costs.

TREAT PEOPLE WITH DISABILITIES
AS YOU WOULD WANT TO BE TREATED

We're often uncertain about how to act when we see or meet someone with a disability. Because we're focusing on the differences between us, we aren't sure we know how people with disabilities want to be treated. It would help if we concentrated more on what we have in common. When we're out in public, we all want to be dealt with politely, to have our privacy respected, and to go about our business without interference. What causes disability and difference is beyond any of our control: an auto accident, genetics, a fall, one bad moment at birth. None of us chooses to have a disability. And any of us could become disabled. If we focus on our shared needs, emotions, and vulnerabilities, we'll feel more at ease with whomever we encounter.

REMINDERS

⊚ Speak to a person with a disability as you'd like to be spoken to, even if you feel uncomfortable at first; be friendly, businesslike, or whatever is called for.

⊚ Don't ask embarrassing personal questions or talk about someone with a disability as though he or she weren't there. Speak directly to the person, not to his or her companion. Talk as you normally do, not loudly or slowly as if the person can't hear or understand.

⊚ When you see someone with a disability, don't stare, but also don't automatically look away. If you would make eye contact, smile, or talk with another person in a similar circumstance, do so with a person who has a disability. If you would simply continue on your way, do that.

⊚ Never point at, talk publicly about, or mock someone, for any reason. Teach your children to be similarly restrained and respectful.

⊚ If someone appears to need help, offer assistance in a matter-of-fact way.

CHAPTER 11

We value our active pursuits as much for the diversion and escape they provide as for the enjoyment they give us. We get through many of life's stresses by planning breaks, entertainment, and adventures for ourselves. As long as we can look forward to an evening walk, weekend softball, a ticket to a concert or football game, or a yearly vacation, we can put up with the pressure of our obligations and hectic routines.

Often, we see leisure activities as our chance to be free, to shed some of the rules and inhibitions that normally limit us. We may feel that we've earned the right, for a short while, to concentrate on our own desires and needs. When we're relaxing or pursuing active enjoyment, we simply want to have fun, without having to worry about, or be inconvenienced by, others.

Yet we rarely can — or even want to — pursue our active interests alone. We need partners, teams, and fans for many sports. When we travel, we go with companions or groups. We voluntarily join crowds at movies, shows, concerts, or sporting events. In fact, the presence of a crowd often enhances our enjoyment as we get caught up in group emotions, strike up casual conversations with strangers, and feel part of a temporary community focused on having a good time.

Getting along with teammates, partners, companions, and strangers is an important part of being active. The more seamless and courteous our interactions with others, the freer we are to concentrate on our activities without the distractions of misunderstandings, frayed tempers, and spoiled arrangements.

Many of our leisure-time dealings with other people involve logistics and practical matters. We need to be considerate about coming to practices on time, making room for others on bike paths and in swim lanes, taking our fair turn in concession lines, sharing court and field time, being quiet during movies and plays, and, when we travel, not intruding on the strangers with whom we share transportation.

As participants in sports, we have to balance our competitiveness with a need to show good sportsmanship, whether we win or lose. This is often difficult, especially when we've invested significant time and effort in training and practice, or when we feel a great deal depends on the outcome of a game or match. The Golden Rule can help to guide our actions in competitive situations and encourage us to act the way we want our partners, teammates, and opponents to act. We all play to win, but we also expect to be treated fairly and with at least basic civility.

One recreational activity that tests many of us is watching our children participate in team sports. We're often too emotionally involved to be mere spectators, particularly if we think our children have been mistreated or have made a mistake. At one extreme, parents yell at their own child. "Can't you even kick a ball!?" At the other extreme, they yell at the opposing team, coaches, or officials. "Are you blind? That was a foul!"

For our children's sake and for our own equilibrium, we have to show self-control and conduct ourselves with the fairness and goodwill we'd like to see in other parent-spectators. Being anything other than a supportive, encouraging voice sets an example of poor sportsmanship and is almost always embarrassing in retrospect. Here, as in our other active pursuits, we need to act in a way that enhances our own and other people's enjoyment. We may feel hemmed in by having to compromise and be considerate. But we'll ultimately have a much better time if our interactions with each other are cordial and calm.

BE THE GOOD SPORT YOU WOULD
LIKE YOUR OPPONENTS TO BE

Some of us are naturally competitive—every game, from Monopoly to volleyball

to golf, is fiercely fought. Others of us are uncomfortable with too much competi-

tion and don't like being seriously challenged. Because it's difficult to change this

aspect of our character, a mismatch of intensity can leave us and our opponents

feeling frustrated and angry. We'll have more enjoyable times if we play primarily

with people who are similar to us in ability and competitiveness. When this isn't

possible, we can try to adjust to the style of our opponents. And if a game is not

as competitive or relaxed as we'd like, we can still find value in the diversion, the

physical activity, and the company.

REMINDERS

* If you play friendly games or matches, be cordial and good-natured with teammates and opponents.
* Be a responsible, supportive team member; do what's good for the group. Praise your teammates' nice work; don't be harsh if they make a mistake.
* If you win in a competitive setting, show your pleasure but avoid gloating or saying anything negative about your opponents in public. Act according to the customs of the sport—shake hands, give a pat on the back, or say a few words.
* When calls go against you during a competitive game, attempt to stay focused and in control; don't show tantrum-like anger. If you lose, be civil and do what's customary for the sport. Offer congratulations if it's expected.
* Try to maintain perspective when competing. You can consider a game or match to be very important, yet still see it as a small event in the scope of everything you'll experience.

TREAT FANS AND AUDIENCE MEMBERS THE WAY YOU WANT TO BE TREATED

As part of a crowd or audience, we want to get absorbed and involved in the game, concert, show, or movie we've come to see. Almost always, the people around us share our interest and our desire to have an enjoyable time. Yet getting along with strangers in the close quarters of a stadium or theater takes restraint and cooperation. We have to consider the comfort of those seated nearby when we talk or move around, and we have to calm ourselves down when strangers irritate us. It may help to remember that most people don't mean to be annoying and that sometimes we may also be a bother. In a crowd, we should do what we can to keep ourselves and others from getting upset; then we can focus on our main activity and on having fun.

REMINDERS

❋ Be courteous and avoid intruding on other fans. It's fine to start a casual conversation as long as it seems welcomed, but be sensitive to people's desire for privacy and space.

❋ Follow each sport's protocol — its accepted forms of politeness — for audience behavior. For instance, football fans cheer all during play; tennis fans don't.

❋ Stay in control. If you're watching a competitive sport, don't get so carried away that you verbally attack rival fans, players, or officials. Don't use offensive language or drink too much.

❋ At symphony concerts, plays, and movies, avoid making noise or moving around. Many audience members are bothered by whispering, fidgeting, excessive coughing, rustling candy wrappers, and electronic devices.

❋ Be considerate of people's sight lines. Don't stand, sit forward, or let your children get up in their seats without checking if those behind you can see.

BE THE KIND OF TRAVELER YOU WOULD LIKE TO ENCOUNTER

When we travel, we enter someone else's home territory. While we're on vacation, the people whose community we're visiting are working and going about their everyday routines. This is part of the charm of traveling; we can see and even immerse ourselves, if we wish, in the daily life of an unfamiliar place. But we also have a responsibility not to interfere with or disrupt the flow of normal activities. We can take our cues from the people and environment and try to fit in as much as possible. In our manner, words, and attitudes, we can show the interest and courtesy we'd like to receive from visitors to our own cities and towns.

REMINDERS

* Be considerate of others on planes, buses, ships, and trains. The more crowded, uncomfortable, or prolonged the trip, the more important it is to be courteous. Avoid disturbing others and taking up extra room.

* Have a pleasant, cooperative demeanor as you tour unfamiliar areas. Don't be loud or boisterous. If you travel out of the country, try to observe and copy customary behavior in restaurants and stores and on public transportation.

* Respect your physical surroundings. Keep your hotel room relatively clean; straighten up after yourself in public; don't do any damage to places you visit.

* Be courteous and friendly to people who serve you in hotels and restaurants. Express your thanks; don't be demanding or act superior.

* Adopt an attitude of curiosity toward unfamiliar things. Try new foods, and enjoy seeing different ways of acting and dressing. Be patient when there are language differences.

CHAPTER 12

In our hurried, hectic lives, we rarely take care of ourselves in other than small, easy ways. We may meet a friend for coffee, buy ourselves a present, or go to a movie. But we don't give thought and attention to our physical, intellectual, and spiritual well-being. We have many reasons, conscious and not, for neglecting our needs: we put others first, feel unworthy, are preoccupied, or don't recognize the necessity. Whatever the causes, we often end up feeling adrift, unable to evaluate our actions and unsure of our beliefs.

To improve the quality of our life, we don't have to add items to our schedule or take attention away from our children and spouse. We can make a positive change by applying the Golden Rule in a personal way, treating ourselves as we would want others to treat us — as though our ideas and feelings were important, and as though we were worthy of concern and respect. In general, we need to make the kinds of well-considered, healthy choices for ourselves that we want our loved ones to make for themselves.

An important part of treating ourselves well is making good use of our time and opportunities. This doesn't mean we have to be continually productive. It does mean we shouldn't waste our time in unexamined routines, passively waiting for better things to happen. We miss many chances for fulfillment when we tell ourselves that our real life will start when we're married or making good money or when all our problems are solved. The years go by, regardless of how we spend them; each year is as valuable and irreplaceable as the ones before and after.

We also do ourselves an injustice when we spend our time dwelling on the unfairness of our situation and on regrets over what we don't have and what we haven't done. While we can't simply will unhappiness away, we can be of two minds about it. On the one hand, we can feel bad for lacking the love, money, or job we want. But we can also accept that this life is all we have. We can choose to do our best with what we've been given and live as fully as possible, whatever our limitations. Such acceptance isn't easy, but we have no real choice if we're to move on and find any satisfaction and pleasure.

To be good to ourselves, we also need to keep hope and optimism in our life, just as we'd want our loved ones to. When we can't look forward either to continued happiness or to change, our negative feelings color all our experiences and strongly affect those around us. With a positive attitude, we can find a way to make our circumstances better, if not materially, then by improving our relationships or changing our behavior, outlook, or perspective.

With the help of the Golden Rule, we can recognize and appreciate what we have now and work to preserve what's good in our lives. We don't need a serious illness, accident, or advancing age to make us value each day and blessing. We can love, treasure, and help our family and friends. We can enjoy and try to take care of the natural beauty around us. We can be grateful for and nurture our useful skills and active mind. And no matter what the state of our health, we can try to take good care of our bodies. If we treat ourselves the way we want others to treat us—and the way we want those we care about to treat themselves—our personal choices will inevitably become more practical, thoughtful, and wise.

TREAT YOUR BODY WELL

We all notice those who have beautiful faces and bodies. But we can get into physical and psychological trouble if we try too hard to compete with or copy these people. Physical beauty is rare and just one of the many arenas in which individuals can shine. We could also pursue knowledge, art, athletics, nurturing, business sense, socializing, inventiveness, and on and on. We all know friends, acquaintances, or public figures who have no more than average looks, yet who are sought after and successful in any number of ways: socially, romantically, professionally. We would be happier and healthier if we chose these talented, self-confident people as our models, and simply admired, rather than chased, physical perfection.

REMINDERS

⊙ Take care of your body, even if you're young, strong, and not concerned about illness. If it's hard to worry about your future well-being, consider the immediate rewards of exercising and eating nutritiously—a healthier appearance, more energy, and fewer minor injuries and ills.

⊙ Pay enough attention to your looks so that your grooming and style don't get in the way of your professional or personal life.

⊙ Avoid taking unnecessary risks with your body; don't use harmful substances or engage in reckless behavior.

⊙ If you become ill or injured, research your condition so you can evaluate and understand what your doctors and others say. Use libraries, computer resources, reference books, and hotlines.

⊙ See doctors or therapists when you have a problem, but ask questions and don't automatically accept what you hear; seek other opinions.

ENGAGE YOUR MIND

Our world is so rich and full of ideas and activities that we can never run out of interesting things to do and think about. Usually, only habit keeps us from trying new creative and intellectual pursuits. We may be watching TV all evening, listening to just one type of music, or avoiding books and computers because that's what we've always done. It can take willpower to break out of our routine. But the more we exercise our mind, the more stimulating, healthy, and rewarding our life will be. When we're mentally active and engaged, we can satisfy our curiosity, find new knowledge and enjoyment, and acquire a deeper understanding of the people, processes, and events that touch us.

REMINDERS

- Reawaken old interests — an instrument you used to play, a collection you set aside — and pursue new ones. Investigate any hobby or field you're curious about; get actively involved or simply talk and read about the subject.
- Be selective about which and how many TV shows you watch. Don't let passive viewing be your main source of stimulation; don't watch simply to fill your days or to have a substitute for relationships and activities.
- Spend time reading, even if you haven't previously enjoyed it. Reading exercises your imagination and offers an easy, portable way to explore any topic at your own pace, in as much depth as you want.
- Involve yourself in creative activities, either as a performer or artist, or as a follower of music, art, drama, dance, or crafts.
- If you're uncomfortable with computers, try to learn basic skills or improve upon what you know; computers can lead you to vast sources of information.

NURTURE YOUR SPIRIT

Our lives are not narrow, though we often focus on small, ordinary things. In truth, we're constant participants in awe-inspiring events: the mysteries of birth and death, our fierce love for family, the strength and beauty of nature, the flow of history, and the power of faith. If we bring a greater awareness of these forces into our daily routines, we'll feel more prepared to appreciate or accept the profound joys and sorrows we experience. We'll feel a stronger connection to people everywhere, to the past and future, and to the natural and spiritual world. And we'll think more clearly about what we hope to accomplish and what we've done so far with the time we've been given.

REMINDERS

- Bring important ideas into your daily life. Think and talk to family and close friends about ethics, tradition, spirituality, history, creativity, and nature.
- At times, talk about death, even if you're uncomfortable. We often feel disconnected from it, as though it were strange and unnatural. Discussing death more openly might help us to view it as natural and inevitable.
- Make the practice of your religion a regular part of your life. However, don't impose your beliefs on others. Show strong respect for different religions and opinions about faith.
- Be wary of trendy, potentially exploitative spirituality. Religious and ethical systems that have stood the tests of time offer faith, connection, and wisdom.
- Try to live according to your values and beliefs so you can reflect on your actions with pride. Treat others well, cherish your loved ones, feel pleased with your good efforts, and appreciate the blessings of this world.

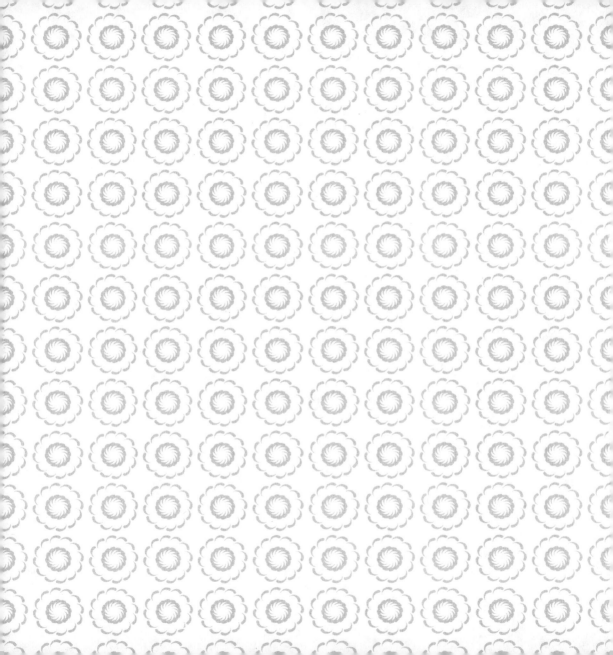